It's a Divine Done Deal

Affirmative Prayers for Easy Living
and Steps to Create Your Own

It's a Divine Done Deal

*Affirmative Prayers for Easy Living
and Steps to Create Your Own*

© 2014 by Nancy Fagen

All rights reserved.

No part of this book may be reproduced or transmitted in any form or by any means, electronic or mechanical, including photocopying, recording, or by any storage and retrieval system, without the written permission of the publisher, except where permitted by law.

Cover Image © Tommy Addison
Author Photo by Sam Jackson

Manufactured in the United States of America

This book is dedicated to the many teachers who have encouraged and inspired me along my life's journey.

Thank you.

Table of Contents

ix   Foreword

xiii   Introduction

1   PART ONE
Affirmative Prayers and Scenarios of Effective Use

- 3 Health
- 7 Prosperity
- 11 Creativity
- 13 Relationships

15   PART TWO
Creating Affirmative Prayers Step by Step

- 19 I Live in Optimal Health
- 21 I Live Prosperously
- 23 I Live in Unlimited Creativity
- 25 I Live in Love and Gratitude

27   PART THREE
Affirmative Prayers for Your Use

- 29 I Accept My Greater Good
- 30 I Affirm Life
- 31 I Am On Purpose
- 32 I Am a Divine Idea
- 33 I Am a Positive Co-creator

34 I Am Centered in the Mind of God
35 I Am Enough
36 I Am in Tune with Divine Nudges of Spirit
37 I Am One with the One
38 I Am Open to the Magic of My Soul
39 I Am Opulence in Action
40 I Am Perfect Health
41 I Am True Success
42 I Am Wide Awake to My Good
43 I Bask in the Presence of Spirit
44 I Bring Forth My Inner Essence of Life
45 I Celebrate My Essential Self
46 I Celebrate the One Life
47 I Circulate My Good
48 I Claim My Good
49 I Deepen My Spiritual Awareness
50 I Ease into This Day
51 I Enjoy Being Alive
52 I Expand My Sense of Self
53 I Expect the Best
54 I Express My True Self
55 I Gratefully Bless All
56 I Honor and Express My Uniqueness
57 I Joyfully Play the Game of Life
58 I Joyfully Live in This Present Moment
59 I Joyously Embrace My Divine Potential
60 I Joyously Express My Inner Splendor
61 I Listen to My Intuition

62 I Live Fearlessly
63 I Live in Calm Assurance
64 I Live in Clarity and Right Action
65 I Live in Divine Clarity
66 I Live in Divine Order
67 I Live in Divine Potential
68 I Live in Ease and Grace
69 I Live in Ease
70 I Live in Endless Sufficiency
71 I Live in Heartfelt Gratitude
72 I Live in Infinite Potential
73 I Live in Limitless Time
74 I Live in Love and Gratitude
75 I Live in Newness
76 I Live in Optimal Health
77 I Live in Peace, Harmony, and Balance
78 I Live in Self-trust
79 I Live in Spiritual Fitness
80 I Live in Sufficiency
81 I Live in the Divine Flow of Life
82 I Live in the Divine Flow of Spirit
83 I Live in the Now
84 I Live in the Oneness of Spirit
85 I Live in the Reality of Spirit
86 I Live in Tune with the Infinite
87 I Live in Unlimited Creativity
88 I Live in New Beginnings
89 I Live Intelligently

90   I Live Limitlessly
91   I Live My Life Lightly
92   I Live Prosperously
93   I Live with a Prosperous Heart
94   I Lovingly Nurture Myself
95   I Make Up My Mind
96   I Realize My Spiritual Strength
97   I Say Yes to Life
98   I Simplify and Glorify My Life
99   I Step Boldly into Freedom
100 I Stretch My Spiritual Muscles
101 I Wisely Follow My Intuition
102 I Wisely Set My Truest Intentions
103 I Wisely Steer Myself Toward My Greater Good
104 I Wisely Work With the Law
105 My Life is Unfolding Perfectly
106 Peace is My Way

107   PART FOUR
Appendices
   109 Steps for Creating Your Personal Prayer
   111 A User-friendly Checklist

113 A Reminder of Your Importance
115 About the Author
117 Acknowledgements
119 Contact Information

Foreword

My spiritual awakening began in 1983 while journeying in Australia. Since then I have experienced many methods of spiritual practice, all of which have had value in my life. However, none have been as deeply beneficial and lasting as the form of affirmative prayer I learned in the summer of 1984 at the Center for Positive Living in Miami.

Now, my life literally revolves around my prayer practice. I begin most every day, whether at home or traveling, engaging in the specific practice of knowing for myself and many others the very highest and best outcome possible. My prayers include my beloved wife who joins me in this practice when I am at home, members of my spiritual community, colleagues and their spiritual communities in and through our spiritual movement, and a variety of others who have asked for my support in consciousness.

I am told that when I do this work, I impress my thought upon the Mind of God, which in turn creates a demonstration according to my thought. Hearing from individuals who report changes in conditions that align with my prayers, I have ample indication that this is so. But, what I know with absolute certainty is that my prayers have a very real and direct impress on how I experience my life. Clear thought accepted, embraced, and embodied through my prayer practice consistently manifests into form in my life.

If this is true for me, the same outcome must be available to everyone. I have no powers above or beyond anyone else. I simply apply a deep inner knowing as I think, say, hear, and envision the outcome I desire. I do this with a loving heart and a clear awareness of the Divine Presence that animates my life.

I always use five steps to guide my awareness. As best I can, I become aware of Infinite Presence as absolute and transcendent. I identify my highest Self within and as that Presence. I realize that what I seek to experience in life is already fully present and available to me right now. From that powerful awareness, I accept and experience deep and abiding gratitude. Then I let go of all the details, relevant or not, and open my life to Divine revelation.

Through this profoundly valuable practice, I can always find God in every circumstance, and I always become more aware of my Divine nature in every experience.

In *It's a Divine Done Deal: Affirmative Prayers for Easy Living and Steps to Create Your Own,* Dr. Nancy Fagen shares the essential value of this spiritual practice in three ways:

First, she shares real-life scenarios and the affirmative prayers used to manifest vibrant health, increased prosperity, harmonious relationships, and creative expression.

Second, she teaches how to create an effective prayer practice that will consistently demonstrate desired results.

Third, she includes a collection of affirmative prayers that can be used to create virtually any desired outcome.

This book will inspire you, but more importantly, it will teach you how to pray clearly, effectively, and from your heart. Thank you, Nancy, for sharing this powerful practice with the world.

Reverend Doctor John B. Waterhouse
President, Centers for Spiritual Living
Author, Five Steps to Freedom

Introduction

I prayed and prayed and prayed and nothing happened. Have you ever experienced this? Have you ever wondered what would happen if there were a way to pray that is effective in getting the results you desire? This book provides affirmative prayers for your use and presents tools for you to create your own, resulting in a life of ease and grace for yourself and the world.

What is affirmative prayer? Affirmative prayer, also referred to as spiritual mind treatment or effective prayer, clears and changes our thoughts and feelings to put us in tune with our chosen desires. It leads the mind to that state of consciousness in which we accept what we wish to believe. Ernest Holmes in *The Science of Mind* wrote, "Prayer, which is a mental act, must accept its own answer as an image in mind before the Divine energies play upon it and make it productive."

You may ask yourself, "How do I know if what I desire is right or wrong for me?" The criterion suggested by Dr. Holmes is, "Does the thing I wish to do express more life, more happiness, more peace to myself, and at the same time harm no one? If it does, it is right. It is not selfish. But if it is done at the expense of anyone, then in such degree you are making a wrong use of the Law."

What is the Law? "The Law is the creative medium of Spirit. Whatever we think, believe in, feel, visualize, vision, image, read, talk about, in fact, all processes which affect or impress us at all, are going into the subjective state of our thought, which is our individualized use of Universal Mind. The Law is a blind force, and whatever goes into the subjective state of our thought tends to return again as some condition." (*The Science of Mind*, Holmes)

By coming from a sense of wholeness, we become magnets which draw from the invisible realms of limitless substance and attract to us who we are in consciousness—the sum total of our thoughts and feelings.

I lovingly support you as you listen to your intuition and know that you need not go through life unguided or living less than your highest potential. Know that you are an individualized expression of the One Power and Presence and in the consciousness of this unity you are privileged to clarify your desires, accept them, give thanks for them and release them into Universal

Law as a Divine Done Deal. Claim your desired good now. You deserve it!

*In spiritual support,
Reverend Nancy Fagen, Ph.D.*

Part One

Affirmative Prayers and Scenarios of Effective Use

Health

A woman in my community was diagnosed as having diabetes and came to me for spiritual counseling. I suggested that she change her terminology from "having diabetes" to "experiencing the diagnosis of diabetes."

I pointed out that by using the word "having" she was claiming this condition as hers and thinking of it as permanent. I suggested she think of this diagnosis as an experience she was going through, thus placing in mind that it is movable and dismissible.

I gave her the following affirmative prayer for her use:

Quote of Theme:

"A definition of health solely on the basis of body diagnosis is incomplete. You are mind, acting through body, in a world which you can always change. People are doing it all the time."

Raymond Charles Barker, *You Can Be Healthy Today*

I Am Perfect Health

Recognizing the One Power and Presence in Its entirety and knowing I am One with It, I confidently speak my word that I am now and always the consciousness of perfect health.

I do not entertain nor do I have interest in thoughts hinting in any degree of the necessity or existence of struggle, indecision, obstruction, unknowingness, imperfection, limitation or disease. Calmly and firmly I refuse to experience any sense of hurry, worry, anxiety, burden or guilt.

My healthy thinking manifests as healthy living. Every cell in my body is vibrant and energized, functioning perfectly. I now peacefully move forward, comfortable with experiencing a greater lightness in living. At ease with myself and all of life, I live in perfect balance and harmony.

Accepting perfect health as the truth of my being, I live easily and naturally in a joyous consciousness. I am grateful this is true, and with calm assurance I now release this truth into Divine Mind and let it be. And so it is.

A few months later, this woman had changed her diet to reflect her healthy thinking, released unnecessary weight, began enjoying increased interest in life, and received a clean bill of health from her doctor. She began taking classes and learned to create her own affirmative prayers.

She changed her life by changing her thinking—and so can you!

Prosperity

I decided to sell a condo I had lived in from time to time for 30 years. Many well-meaning acquaintances let me know that due to the state of the economy this was not the time to sell. They made sure I knew there was an abundance of condos for sale in the area that were not selling.

I kept my thinking attuned to the fulfillment of my desire and replied with the truth that the sale of my condo had nothing to do with the others for sale and nothing to do with the state of the economy. I affirmed for one perfect buyer who desired to buy my condo at the perfect price and for the perfect terms.

Two weeks after listing my condo the real estate agent contacted me with two offers. One was cash, and very close to the listing price. The other was also very close to the listing price but with terms. I accepted the cash offer.

When the agent presented me with the papers to sign, he said, "Someone up there must like you." I smiled and replied, "Yes, I know." What he did not know was that I had been praying affirmatively for my good in the form of the perfect sale to come to me in the perfect time, at the perfect price, and I had gratefully released this prayer to the Universe knowing it had already happened.

The affirmative prayer I used:

Quote of the Theme:

"All is Good and all is God because It draws and pushes and moves me on ... There is good for me, and I ought to have it."

Emma Curtis Hopkins,
Scientific Christian Mental Practice

I Claim My Good

All is Good and all is God. Rejoicing that I am a living, breathing, individualized expression of Good, of God, I gratefully allow It to express in Its entirety in, through, and as me. It is who I am.

Living my life in an open, receptive mode of being, I easily attract, joyously welcome, and fully embrace the good now coming to me and the greater good yet to come. Grateful I am a magnet for good, I delight that only good comes to me *and only good goes from me. I am a receiving and giving center for increasing good as I allow it to move into all areas of my life, showing up as opulent wealth, optimal health, loving relationships, and unlimited creativity. Being filled and overflowing with goodness, I naturally and peacefully influence my world of effects, exuding good and greater good to all. It is my chosen way of being in the world.*

Delighted this truth is now a reality for me, I rejoice as I allow it to be. I claim my good, and so it is.

Creativity

One of the ways we can use our creative nature is to think out of the box of preconceived ideas. One woman shared her dilemma about accepting a job she desired that would not leave her free on Sundays to participate in spiritual activities. She said she liked everything else about the offer but was leaning strongly toward refusing the interview.

I suggested she accept the interview and simply ask if it would be possible to change the work day scheduled on Sunday to a different day. Much to her delight, the interviewer agreed to replace the Sunday work day with another day in the week. She accepted the job and is very grateful for it, and for the schedule. All this took was her willingness to see the possibility of a different schedule and accept that in her mind as a possibility.

Here is an affirmative prayer that addresses living in expanded thinking and refusing to accept limiting ideas:

Quote of Theme:

"The Mind of God is Infinite. The mind of man[kind]

is some part of the Infinite, Creative Mind of God. Therefore the mind of man[kind] is as infinite as is man[kind's] capacity to understand his true relationship to God or Spirit."

Ernest Holmes, *The Science of Mind*

I Live in Infinite Potential

In the awareness of oneness with the One Power and Presence, I live in the consciousness of Infinite Potential, opening my mind to new vistas of living.

As I align my thoughts and feelings with expanded possibilities, I allow myself to see new visions and ways of being in the world. I open to Infinite Mind moving through, in, and as me, creating within me a greater consciousness of peace, harmony, joy, creativity, prosperity, and love.

Knowing that I live in Infinite Potential, I refuse to accept any limiting ideas of myself or others. I gently embody my new world in ease and grace without any sense of struggle or strain. As I live in my ever-expanding potential, I joyously embrace the delightful effects of my new thinking as it shows up in my world.

Accepting this truth as being completed in Divine Mind, I gratefully let it be so. And so it is.

Relationships

Is loving myself selfish? There was a time in my life when I did not realize that I must love myself first in order to give love to others. Through knowing my true nature as the individualization of the One Power and Presence, I came to the understanding that by loving myself I was really loving the Divine expressing in, through, and as me.

Since we really are all one, by loving myself I spread more love to everyone. I am reminded of the phrase, "Love your neighbor as yourself," attributed to Jesus the Christ. One day I realized it did not say "instead" of yourself.

The first place to start an unconditional loving relationship is with myself. Then, and only then, am I able to unconditionally love others. As I lift myself up by loving myself unconditionally, I am able and willing to enjoy unconditional loving relationships with all those in my world.

An affirmative prayer for loving relationships:

Quote of Theme:

"When you meditate, open not only your listening mind but the other door of your mind as well so that eternal love streams out as fast as it comes in."

Mary Strong, *Letters of the Scattered Brotherhood*

I Live in the Divine Flow of Life

I am one with the eternal stream of Life flowing throughout all existence. Living in the realization of this unity, I embrace who I am, rejoicing in the Presence of the Divine Flow of Life individualized in, through, and as me. In this sacred awareness, I now unhesitatingly move confidently forward in the perfect expression of right action. True to my God nature, I express love and light in ways that bless all.

Being led by Spirit to easily and courageously create the perfect world of effects, I allow neither fear nor doubt to enter my consciousness. My every action is sanctioned by Divine Source as I naturally and easily experience and express the eternal stream of love. I intelligently guide the direction of my talents to the highest and greatest good, joyfully offering uplifting and nurturing inspiration from the ever-flowing, constant current of Life to myself and all those in my world.

Living in the Divine flow of Life, I joyously, freely, and lovingly express who I am. I rejoice in this truth, and let it be. And so it is.

Part Two

Creating Affirmative Prayers Step-by-Step

An affirmative prayer is a means of changing our thoughts and feelings so that the Universal Power—which always says "yes"—has a clear impression of how to respond to us. Affirmative prayer is not asking or pleading to an outside god or force. Rather, it is clearly stating and knowing that whatever you have claimed is yours now. The more feeling and emotion you express, the more effective your prayer.

In *Creative Mind and Success*, Ernest Holmes wrote:

> *We sit down with our own souls, at peace with the world, at peace with ourselves; we realize that we are dealing with something that is a reality, something that cannot fail. We get a clear concept of the thing; we rest in that realization while the Universal Creative Power takes it up and acts upon it. We have stated just what we wanted done unto us; we have believed; we have believed that we have received; never again will we contradict the fact that we have stated. The person who can do this is sure of getting results.*

Notice that in the affirmative prayers in this book, there is a consistent pattern. As you create your own prayers you may choose to follow these examples. Let me suggest that you always use first person "I," "myself," or "me" as you create your prayers. Also, by staying in the present tense, using the word "now" instead of "will," you invite the Universe to establish your desire in your mind and heart as being already present in this moment, attracting it to you.

Following is an outline of suggested steps of affirmative prayer. If there is no thought of an obstacle, steps of Denying and Reaffirming may be eliminated.

Recognizing. *Divine Intelligence is all there is.*

Unifying. *I am an individualized expression of It.*

Accepting. *I now accept my stated desired good.*

Denying. *There is no obstacle to my desired good.*

Reaffirming. *I totally accept my desired good.*

Expressing thanks. *I am deeply grateful this is so.*

Releasing. *I let go, knowing it is done. And so it is.*

Notice that these steps are often blended together rather than stated entirely separately. As you create your own affirmative prayers, use your own unique style, keeping the essence of the formula as a guide.

Following are examples of affirmative prayers I have written to address the areas of health, prosperity, creativity, and relationships.

Health

Quote of the theme (optional):

"The spiritual [person] needs no healing, health is an omnipresent reality, and when the obstructions that hinder healing are removed, it will be found that health was there all the time. So in your work, do not feel that you must heal anyone. Your only responsibility is to uncover the Truth."

Ernest Holmes, The Science of Mind

Title
I Live in Optimal Health

Recognizing
Recognizing the One Power and Presence is all there is, I joyfully unify with It in Its entirety.

Unifying
In this consciousness of unity I embrace the perfect expression of who I am—an individualized expression of the One.

Accepting
I allow this perfection to express fully in, through, and as me as perfect health. Every cell in my body is functioning perfectly, resulting in perfect assimilation, perfect circulation, and perfect elimination. My life is one of energetic vitality expressing in balance, harmony, and peace.

Denying Any Obstacle
Keeping my consciousness clear of any disturbance, I allow nothing to interfere with the perfect workings of my mind, emotions, and body.

Reaffirming Total Acceptance
Every part of my body continually regenerates, keeping perfect harmony and balance as the natural state of my being and showing up in my world of effects as unbounded vitality and free flowing energy.

Expressing Gratitude and **Releasing**
Grateful that this is now so, I release this truth as it manifests in my life. I live in optimal health. And so it is.

Prosperity

Quote of the theme (*optional*):

"…the word 'prosperity' in its root means 'wholeness' …the spiritual laws of wholeness, when practiced, bring peace, health and plenty into our lives."

    Catherine Ponder, *The Dynamic Laws of Prosperity*

Title
I Live Prosperously

Recognizing
The One Power and Presence is everywhere present in all Its totality.

Unifying
I am one with It. In this consciousness of unity, I am grateful that Creative Intelligence easily and clearly demonstrates in perfect ways that which I impress upon It.

Accepting
I now accept, without any obstruction or delay, a reality of prosperous living.

Denying Any Obstacle
Any thoughts in my conscious or unconscious mind that may negate the perfect manifestation of a joyous and opulent life are peacefully and completely dissolved into the nothingness where they belong.

Reaffirming Total Acceptance
Cooperating with Spiritual Law, I maintain a consciousness of peace, health, and prosperity. My relationships are loving and supportive, my self-expression flows creatively and joyously, my supply is constant and abundant, and my health reflects perfect wholeness and wellbeing.

Expressing Gratitude and **Releasing**
Grateful that my word is Truth, I rejoice as I allow it to be so. I live prosperously. And so it is.

Creativity

Quote of the theme (optional):

"This is how creativity happens—when the mind is fertile; when everything is seen as having value and each event is welcomed as an opportunity; when strange and unforeseen accidents are met with confidence; when the unpredictable dance of life, rather than causing fear or annoyance, stimulates interest; and when there is always a 'why' to ask, always a game to play."

Piero Ferrucci, *Inevitable Grace*

Title
I Live in Unlimited Creativity

Recognizing and **Unifying**
Being one with the Creator of all things, I joyously individualize the ever-flowing, never-ending Life of unlimited creativity.

Accepting
I keep my mind clear and fertile, seeing everything as having intrinsic value and every event as an uplifting opportunity.

Denying Any Obstacle
I easily and effectively dismiss any fears or annoyances that appear to be real as I openly embrace my infinite potential, intelligently creating beautiful and bold blessings for myself and all others.

Reaffirming Total Acceptance
With undying confidence, I courageously and fearlessly meet all the effects appearing in my life, knowing that by applying my understanding of universal principles and by perfectly aligning my thoughts and feelings with my desires, I create new experiences resulting in an expanded consciousness of increased opulence, peace, joy, and love.

Expressing Gratitude and **Releasing**
Grateful this is now so, I rejoice as I release this truth into Divine Mind. I live in unlimited creativity. And so it is.

Relationships

Quote of the theme (optional):

"Wouldn't it be wonderful if we could cover the world in the most beautiful of water crystals? How do we go about this? The answer is love and gratitude... If all the people of the world can have love and gratitude, the pristine beauty of the earth will once again return."

Masaru Emoto, The Hidden Messages in Water

Title
I Live in Love and Gratitude

Recognizing, Unifying and **Accepting**
Knowing that all living things exist in a constantly changing state of interconnectedness, and knowing that I am a living influence in the unity of the One Whole, I set my positive intent to live as a spiritual center of love and gratitude, radiating through my consciousness a positive effect upon the world.

Denying Any Obstacle
Anything unlike the harmony of love and gratitude is totally and peacefully dismissed into the nothingness where it belongs.

Reaffirming Total Acceptance
I lay no claim to that which is less than the highest spiritual perfection expressing as my life. As I exude the consciousness of love and gratitude, I live my life to the fullest, naturally and joyously expressing who I am—the perfect personification of unconditional love and unlimited gratitude.

Expressing Gratitude and Releasing
Grateful to the Law which now accepts and manifests this positive intention, I relax into knowing my loving and grateful way of living contributes to upholding the pristine beauty of the world. I live in love and gratitude. And so it is.

Part Three

Affirmative Prayers for Your Use

"Nothing can ever be lost through spiritual release. Instead, your own good and the good of all concerned is much freer to move into your life. Through release, your power of attracting good is greatly increased."

Catherine Ponder,
The Dynamic Laws of Prosperity

I Accept My Greater Good

Knowing I am an individualized expression of God, the All Good, I now accept greater and greater good in my life as a natural effect of my spiritual evolution.

I willingly release from the closets of my consciousness, and the closets of my environment, any clutter or leftovers from my prior thinking. I intelligently and calmly decide what to keep and what to let go. I keep that which nurtures and supports me in moving forward to greater and greater good.

I lovingly bless and gently release that which has served its purpose in my life, whatever it may have been. As I do this, my consciousness is filled and overflowing with clarity, order, and peace.

With gratitude, I now accept my greater good and allow it to be so. And so it is.

"The infinite power of Divinity radiates down through the levels of consciousness like sunlight in the forest. It sustains all life."

David Hawkins, *The Eye of the I*

I Affirm Life

Knowing that everything in my life is created and sustained by the Power and Presence of Spirit, I allow this infinite power of Divinity to permeate me, fill me, and flow through me, spilling over as Spirit-filled energy—the very essence of Life. It is who I am.

From this Spirit-filled place of unity, I easily, peacefully, and knowingly embrace life-affirming choices. I allow into my consciousness only that which totally supports my highest God nature, refusing to entertain anything less than the very best of Life. All my thoughts, decisions, and actions are in perfect alignment with my purpose of expressing as my highest and best in all areas of my living. As I make life-affirming choices, I joyously welcome the magnificent results manifesting as abiding peace, opulent prosperity, unconditional love, optimal health, and unlimited creativity. I rejoice as my wise choices unfold the blessings of Spirit in ways that are visible in my world of effects.

Gratefully releasing this truth to Divine Mind, I relax into accepting that it is now manifest as the deepest reality of my being. I affirm Life. And so it is.

"Too often we travel on cruise control, and the events of our lives flick by like white lines on the freeway, their lessons lost on us."

Gregg Levoy,
Callings: Finding and Following an Authentic Life

I Am On Purpose

There is one Purpose in the Universe. It is Creative Intelligence expressing perfectly in all, through all, and as all. I am a unique expression of this one Purpose as It moves in, through, and as me.

I now align myself with my highest Self-expression in all areas of my life. Staying on purpose in all my thoughts, intentions, and actions, I create my life from an inner knowingness of right thinking and right action. I do not allow myself to stray into self-pity, self-denial, or self-despair. Knowing I am an individualized expression of Spirit, deserving and accepting the very best in life, I refuse to settle for anything less. Being in harmony and in tune with the highest expression of my Divine Self, I radiate joy and lightness in living. Love and laughter fill my world, and wellbeing permeates all my experiences. Everything I think, say, and do is a perfect reflection of my inner delight in being on purpose with the highest expression of who I am.

Gratefully releasing this truth to Divine Mind, I allow it to be. I am on purpose. And so it is.

"We are never left without a witness of the Eternal, and in our greatest moments—in those flash-like visions of mystic grandeur—we know that we are made of eternal stuff, fashioned after a Divine Pattern."

Ernest Holmes, *The Science of Mind*

I Am a Divine Idea

God—the Creator and Sustainer of all Being—is the Intelligence underlying and permeating all that is; thus, I am a Divine idea of this all-powerful, all-knowing, and ever-present Source of All Good as It expresses in, through, and as me.

Acknowledging I am an idea in the mind of God and an eternal expression of the Divine, I honor and respect who I am. I take loving care of my body, nurturing it in all ways. I appreciate my uniqueness, expressing it magnificently. All my relationships are filled and overflowing with warmth and blessings to all in my world. Knowing nothing is too good to be true for me, I live my life in beauty and opulence. Rejoicing in the awareness of who I am, I embrace my infinite potential as I easily and effectively move into greater expression of bountiful ideas that celebrate the wonder of who I am—a Divine idea in the mind of God.

I accept this truth as I gratefully release it into Divine Mind, knowing it is now so. I am a Divine idea. And so it is.

"When we recognize how positive and negative beliefs control our biology, we can use this knowledge to create lives filled with health and happiness. ... my understanding led me to realize the importance of integrating the realms of Spirit and science, which was a radical shift from my background as an agnostic scientist."

Bruce Lipton, The Biology of Belief

I am a Positive Co-creator

I recognize that Spirit is all encompassing in Its entirety in every point of creation, and I rejoice that I am a unified individualization of It.

As I live in this consciousness of unity, I joyfully and naturally create and sustain a positive thought field resulting in a life filled with health, happiness and unlimited good. By consciously and intelligently choosing the highest and best thoughts in all situations I am filled with inspiration, intuitively in tune with my infinite potential as an individualized expression of Infinite Mind. I am led by Spirit to easily accomplish all things necessary for the perfect effect of living a life of wholeness, peace, and joy.

Grateful for these blessings, I release this truth knowing it is complete in Divine Mind. I live in great expectation and undoubting confidence as I allow it to manifest through me. I am a positive co-creator. And so it is.

"The Mind we use is the Mind of the Universe. This is God in man[kind] and it is only through this Mind that we understand anything."

> Ernest Holmes, *The Science of Mind*

I Am Centered in the Mind of God

The Mind of God is where I live, move, and have my being. It is the reality through which the One Life expresses in, through, and as me. In the consciousness of this unity, I allow myself to be saturated and overflowing with the One Power and Presence, individualized as me.

There is no power that can separate me from Its Presence. It is who I am. Disregarding any appearances of duality, I remain centered within the realms of Spirit, trusting the Mind of the Universe to guide me in ways that are for my highest good and the highest good of all in my world.

Relaxing into knowing Universal Mind and my mind are One Mind, I attune myself to the leadings of Spirit. I am alert and attentive to the guidance of my intuition, and I follow its promptings as it leads me in nurturing and productive ways.

Grateful for this knowing, I release these truths into Divine Mind, allowing the Law to manifest Its good through me now. I am centered in the Mind of God. And so it is.

"In the quiet acceptance of 'enoughness now' lies our inner power to choose to be responsible and responsive to life. We put ourselves in the forefront in that way and stop giving our power away to someone or something else that we may consider more enough than us."

Margaret Storz,
I Am Enough & Other Wisdom for Daily Living

I Am Enough

God is all there is; I am an expression of God. God is enough; I am enough. There is nothing else that I could possibly be.

In the oneness of Spirit I accept my "enoughness now" in this moment, spontaneously allowing my belief and feeling of being enough to expand in Infinite potential in ever-widening circles of consciousness. No one or no thing is more enough than I am. In my acceptance of being enough, I exercise my inner power to be responsible and responsive to life in ways that uplift myself and others. At every point of my spiritual evolution I reside in knowing this to be the truth of my being. All my interactions with Life come from a place of fullness—a place of being enough. As the presence of Spirit, I lack for nothing. Because God and I are one, I am enough.

Gratefully, I release this truth into Mind, knowing it is now so. I am enough. And so it is.

"Back of the conflict of ideas, back of the din of external life and action; back, back in the innermost recesses of uplifted thought and silent contemplation, there is a voice… We must learn to listen to this voice. Call it conscience, intuition, or what we will, it is there. No [one] need go unguided through life, for all are Divine at the center and all are Images of the Most High."

Ernest Holmes, *The Science of Mind*

I Am in Tune with Divine Nudges of Spirit

Knowing the One Power and Presence is everywhere present and expresses in Its entirety through, in, and as me, I harmoniously and intuitively live in tune with ever-present Divine Nudges of Spirit.

I am constantly aware of promptings which lead me to unlimited creative expression, optimal health, loving relationships, and opulent living in all areas of my life. Responding intelligently and wisely to Spirit expressing, I move in right directions for my increasing good. I know what to do and willingly move into right action with ease and grace. Clearly responding to my intuitive knowing, I peacefully move forward into more expansive thought, clearly recognizing what is right for me in every moment of every day.

Grateful that I live in tune with Divine Nudges of Spirit, I joyously accept this truth, allowing it to be. And so it is.

"...a voice resounds throughout my consciousness with the roar of thunder. You are God, you say, and then, and then, you say, You are Me! What? You are Me! ...This takes a lot of believing."

Jack Addington, *The Joy of Meditation*

I Am One with the One

Recognizing the One Power and Presence from which all things emerge, I joyfully embrace the truth of my unity with It. I am one with the One, resonating with the vibrations of being in tune with the Infinite.

In the consciousness of this sacred unity, I know and feel the magnificence of Spirit expressing in, through, and as me. Opening to the infinite possibilities that lie before me, I release any regrets of the past, any hesitations or indecisions of the present, and any fears of the future. I relax into trusting Universal Law to respond to my intentions as I confidently and easily create and sustain my life in harmony, peace, and balance.

Firm in the belief that I am one with the One, I allow the realization of this truth to permeate and saturate all aspects of my life. In gratitude and joy I live in the magnificent Oneness with Spirit. And so it is.

"The magic of the soul is the spiritual alchemy—the art of transforming the world of form through the power of Spirit. By opening to the magic of spiritual reality, we bring the magic of our souls into our everyday lives."

Patrick J. Harbula, *The Magic of the Soul*

I Am Open to the Magic of My Soul

Knowing I am expressing the One Power and Presence existing in Its entirety in all time and space, I allow It to flow in, through and as me. In this moment of awareness I still myself to the magic of my soul, experiencing the fullness and richness of who I am.

Being aware of the beauty, peace, and love vibrantly living within me and surrounding me, I allow this awareness to enrich and enhance my perception of the magical qualities of my world. I am flexible and changeable to my infinite potential and to new possibilities, knowing that I am led by Spirit to easily and peacefully accomplish all things necessary for the manifestation of my desires.

Realizing the magic of spiritual reality as the truth of my being, I joyfully bring the magic of my soul into my everyday life. I am grateful for this truth, and I let it be. And so it is.

"I now release the gold mine within me. I am linked with an endless golden stream of prosperity which comes to me under grace in perfect ways."

Florence Scovel Shinn, *Your Word is Your Wand*

I Am Opulence in Action

There is an eternal flow of unlimited good expressing as the One Power and Presence and it is individualized in, through, and as me. In the unity of this consciousness, I rejoice as I live, move, and have my being in the opulence of Spirit.

I am an irresistible magnet for all that belongs to me by Divine Right. All that I desire, require, and claim is now mine. My world is permeated with ever-present and overflowing good, and I intelligently release my supply through fearless faith and right thinking. Nothing stands in the way of this opulent action. Any belief in lack or debt is now dissipated into the nothingness where it belongs. As I release the gold mine within me, I invite, welcome, and embrace an endless stream of prosperity which now and always comes to me under grace and in perfect ways.

In overflowing gratitude, I know this is the truth of my being. I let go and let the Law bring into my world of visible effects that which I have decreed. I am opulence in action. And so it is.

"A definition of health solely on the basis of body diagnosis is incomplete. You are mind, acting through body, in a world which you can always change. People are doing it all the time."

Raymond Charles Barker, *You Can Be Healthy Today*

I Am Perfect Health

Recognizing the One Power and Presence in Its entirety and knowing I am one with It, I confidently speak my word that I am now and always the consciousness of perfect health.

I do not entertain, nor do I have interest in, thoughts hinting in any degree of the necessity or existence of struggle, indecision, obstruction, unknowingness, imperfection, limitation or disease. Calmly and firmly, I refuse to experience any sense of hurry, worry, anxiety, burden or guilt. My healthy thinking manifests as healthy living. Every cell in my body is vibrant and energized, functioning perfectly. I now peacefully move forward, comfortable with experiencing a greater lightness in living. At ease with myself and all of life, I live in perfect balance and harmony.

Accepting perfect health as the truth of my being, I live easily and naturally in a joyous consciousness. I am grateful this is true, and with calm assurance I now release this truth into Divine Mind and let it be. I am perfect health. And so it is.

"True success is … the experience of the miraculous. It is the unfolding of the divinity within us."

Deepak Chopra, *The Seven Spiritual Laws of Success*

I Am True Success Now

Recognizing and unifying with the One Power and Presence, I know I am an individualization of It. I rejoice in this knowing, allowing my inner Divinity to naturally, gracefully, and lovingly unfold in all areas.

I express my God-Self in all relationships, knowing the Divine is everywhere present in Its entirety in all people and events. My creative expression flourishes, endlessly flowing from the Source of my being. I am abundantly supplied in opulent ways and with effortless ease. Every cell in my body is functioning perfectly, nurturing and sustaining me as I joyfully express my innate Divine nature.

I perceive the presence of God wherever I go and in whatever I engage. Experiencing my life as miraculous expression at all times, I knowingly live from the essence of the God-Self within. As I unfold to Spirit I increasingly embrace the true meaning of success, claiming greater and greater good in my life.

Naturally, gracefully, and lovingly unfolding to the Divinity within, I give thanks for this truth of my being. I am true success now. And so it is.

"We really lead magic lives, guided and provided for at every step; if we have ears to hear and eyes that see."

Florence Shinn Schovel, *Your Word is Your Wand*

I Am Wide Awake to My Good

The all-encompassing good of the One Power and Presence everywhere present in Its entirety, now expresses in, through, and as me. I am an individualized expression of It.

In this consciousness of unity, I speak my word that I am wide awake to my increasing good, perceiving and expecting wondrous, magical, and opulent experiences in my life this day and every day. Listening and responding to my intuition, I move easily, intelligently, and peacefully in the direction of Divine leadings, prompting me into right action. Knowing the supply of all good is inexhaustible, that Divine substance is everywhere present, I lovingly and generously allow Spirit to express Its good in unlimited ways in, through, and as me.

I am grateful for eyes that see and ears that hear only good as I naturally and joyously live a magical life, guided and provided for every step of my way. Only good comes to me and only good goes forth from me. Fully embracing the good in my life, I release this truth to Universal Law knowing it is now a reality. I am wide awake to my ever-increasing good. And so it is.

"Surely goodness and mercy shall follow me all the days of my life; and I shall dwell in the house of the Lord forever."

A Psalm of David, RSV, *The Bible*

I Bask in the Presence of Spirit

Recognizing the One Power and Presence as all there is, I delight in knowing my life is an individualization of It. In the consciousness of this unity, I bask in the Presence of Spirit, aware there is no opposition to God as the expression of All-Good.

I easily and naturally move into a higher consciousness of living as I experience increased blessings in all areas of my life. I joyfully express my creative nature, attracting new and purposeful ideas that easily and effectively support me in my ongoing spiritual evolution, blessing myself and others in magnificent and wondrous ways. I am graciously filled and generously overflowing with increased love, joy, peace and an everlasting opulent supply of good.

As I relax into my ever-increasing greater good, I rejoice in recognizing and embracing an increased awareness of the omnipresence of Spirit in, through, and as me. Being grateful that this is so, I let it be. I bask in the Presence of Spirit. And so it is.

"Jesus said: When you give rise to that which is within you, what you have will save you. If you do not give rise to it, what you do not have will destroy you."

Stevan Davies (translation), *The Gospel of Thomas*

I Bring Forth My Inner Essence of Light

Knowing the Light of the One God is individualized in, through, and as me, I honor and bring forth the Divine essence of who I am.

Allowing my light to shine, I illumine my world and the world of all. As my inner light emerges, it dissipates any darkness in my life and refuses to allow the illusion of fear or doubt to appear in my consciousness. Fully expressing the Light Being I am, I shine forth gloriously and magnificently, manifesting as joy, peace, harmony, compassion, and love. I let my Light shine into all areas of my world, experiencing increasing expansion and understanding of my Divine potential.

As I bring forth the Divine essence of who I am, I am more alive to the realization of my oneness with Spirit, creating and sustaining a life of increased blessings for myself and others. Grateful this is now so, I release it to Divine Mind and joyfully allow my inner essence of Light to shine in, through, and as me. And so it is.

"Each and every day we are provided stimulus to cultivate our consciousness. Even amidst the crash of breaking worlds—or an economic crisis—that which we are within cannot be taken away. The joy, peace, love, intelligence, bliss, creativity—nothing can diminish our Essential Self. Lean into this truth, affirm it and, above all, practice it."

> Michael Bernard Beckwith, *Meditative Thought*

I Celebrate My Essential Self

In this eternal moment, I celebrate my essential Self as I acknowledge and joyously experience the One Power and Presence expressing in, through, and as me.

I am now and forever in a constant state of peacefully unfolding to the Divine Potential within me, being increasingly aware of Its eternal and harmonious movement in my life. The permanence of that which I am—the individualized expression of Spirit—is the core of my being. I live, move, and allow this Being to fully express as I choose the highest and best choices for my life. Nothing can diminish the qualities of my essential Self for I constantly and easily embrace joy, peace, love, intelligence, bliss, and creativity as my inherent nature.

Delighted that this is true for me, I graciously express my gratitude with overflowing thanksgiving and abundant joy. I celebrate my essential Self. And so it is.

"There is One Life. That Life is God. That Life is Perfect. That Life is my Life now."

Ernest Holmes, Radio Broadcasting Tapes

I Celebrate the One Life

I recognize and celebrate the One Life, knowing It continually creates and sustains all there is. I recognize and celebrate my unique individualization of this One Life, knowing I create and sustain all there is in my world.

In this consciousness of oneness I delight in being an outlet of this One Energy, One Spirit, One Life. I celebrate knowing the Mind, Spirit, and Intelligence I find in myself is of this One Life expressing through me according to my understanding of It. In It I live, move, and have my being. In full acceptance that my life is the One Life expressing in, through and as me, I consciously and wisely direct my thoughts and emotions, keeping them in perfect alignment with what I choose to create. I acknowledge the gifts of Spirit innately residing within my consciousness, and I now freely express them, blessing myself and all others.

As I Celebrate the One Life, I allow appreciation, gratitude, and wellbeing to flow joyously through me into all areas of my life. Gratefully knowing this is now the truth, I let it be so. I celebrate the One Life. And so it is!

"In the order of nature, we cannot render benefits to those from whom we receive them, or only seldom. But the benefit we receive must be rendered again, line for line, deed for deed, cent for cent, to somebody. Beware of holding too much good staying in your hand."

Ralph Waldo Emerson, *Essays*

I Circulate My Good

Knowing there are no limitations in Universal Mind, and knowing I am an individualized expression of It, I recognize I am a Divine conduit through which love, peace, joy, and prosperity freely flow in unlimited measure.

I keep myself clear and flowing in consciousness; there are no obstructions or delays in the circulation of good now coming to me and now going forth from me. As I attract greater and greater good into my life, I gratefully accept the ever-increasing potential and reality of increasing good. Generously I allow all good to flow in, through, and as me into expanding circuits and circles of greater influence and unlimited manifestations. There is no limit to the good I give and receive.

In this moment, I naturally and joyfully circulate the good that I receive and the good that I am. Thankful I am in the flowing currents of Life, I release this truth and allow it to be. I circulate my good. And so it is.

"I am seeking my Good, and my Good is my God, because it draws and pushes and moves me on ... There is good for me, and I ought to have it."

> Emma Curtis Hopkins,
> *Scientific Christian Mental Practice*

I Claim My Good

All is Good and all is God. Rejoicing that I am a living, breathing, individualized expression of Good, of God, I gratefully allow It to express in Its entirety in, through, and as me. It is who I am.

Living my life in an open, receptive mode of being, I easily attract, joyously welcome, and fully embrace the good now coming to me and the greater good yet to come. Grateful I am a magnet for good, I delight that only good comes to me and only good goes from me. I am a receiving and giving center for increasing good as I allow it to move into all areas of my life, showing up as opulent wealth, optimal health, loving relationships, and unlimited creativity. Being filled and overflowing with goodness, I naturally and peacefully influence my world of effects, exuding good and greater good to all. It is my chosen way of being in the world.

Delighted this truth is now a reality for me, I rejoice as I allow it to be. I claim my good, and so it is.

"You find peace not by rearranging the circumstances of your life, but by realizing who you are at the deepest level."

Eckhart Tolle, *Stillness Speaks*

I Deepen My Spiritual Awareness

In the stillness of this moment I immerse myself in the realization of knowing I am one with the One. As I relax into this consciousness of unity, I move into a deeper understanding of my spiritual nature. I joyously feel the presence of Spirit in the stillness of my being, in the action of my thoughts, and in the workings of my body, thus creating a renewed sense of peaceful connectedness with All.

As I deepen my spiritual awareness, increasingly realizing and appreciating I am the One Life individualized, I allow the One Life to fully express in, through, and as me. As I do, I know I am the consciousness through which stillness and peace flow and this knowing manifests in all I say and do. Circumstances of my life automatically rearrange themselves to be in harmony with this deeper spiritual awareness; anything unlike this spiritual truth obliterates into the nothingness that it is.

In gratitude I bask in the light of my ever-deepening spiritual awareness, knowing it is the eternal truth of my being. And so it is.

"Someone has said that courage contains genius and magic. Face a situation fearlessly, and there is no situation to face; it falls away of its own weight."

Florence Scovel Shinn,
The Game of Life and How to Play It

I Ease Into This Day

Knowing that I am an individualized expression of the One Power and Presence in its entirety, I ease into this day, nurturing myself all the way.

Wisely setting my intentions, I allow myself to easily accomplish that which I choose. I move peacefully, effectively, and efficiently in the clear direction of my desires, knowing that any thoughts of hardships or obstacles from the past, present, or future are now dissipated into the nothingness where they belong. Moving forward into total acceptance that the Universe supports me in all ways, I lovingly and peacefully embrace a new vision of unlimited prosperity and purposeful living as I unfold into more and more of my Infinite potential.

I see my desires manifested as I hold firmly to the vision of successful and intelligent living in all areas of my life. Grateful for this knowing, I release my word, now accepting this truth as I ease into this day and every day, nurturing myself all the way. And so it is.

"Life is the action of Spirit. God is never bored. The infinite is forever Mind creating new ideas, new concepts, and new purposes."

Raymond Charles Barker, *The Power of Decision*

I Enjoy Being Alive

The Life of God is my Life now and I express It joyously and spontaneously. It is who I am.

Celebrating my aliveness and wellbeing in Spirit, I exude boundless creativity, expressing it freely. I refuse to be bored or to be content with that which does not interest me. Staying current with my expanding consciousness, I attract people, ideas, and events that stimulate my mind and my heart. As I stay centered in the truth of my ever-expanding spiritual awareness, my external world aligns itself to reflect my consciousness. Opening to the vast array of infinite possibilities that lie before me, I joyously choose new vistas of living perfect for my spiritual fulfillment. As I move forward into what nurtures me, my aliveness increasingly flourishes. Each moment of each day I experience more and more enjoyment of being alive in Spirit.

Delighted that this is the truth of my being, I gratefully release my word into Divine Mind, knowing it is now so as I willingly allow it to work through me. I enjoy being alive. And so it is.

"Your ability to spontaneously fulfill your desires is directly proportional to your experience of your non-local self."

Deepak Chopra, *The Spontaneous Fulfillment of Desire: Harnessing the Infinite Power of Coincidence*

I Expand My Sense of Self

Recognizing the One Power and Presence is everywhere present in Its entirety, and knowing I am an individualized expression of It, I now consciously choose to expand the experience of my sense of Self.

I open myself to a greater understanding and acceptance of Infinite Potential as I identify with the all-knowing, all-powerful, everywhere-present qualities of Spirit. As I open myself, the awareness of my local self expands to fully embrace its oneness with the non-local, all-encompassing Self. Expanding my experience of Self, I enhance and embrace the spontaneous fulfillment of my desires, creating blessings for myself and others.

Any thought or feeling of unworthiness or impossibility is immediately and totally dismissed into the nothingness where it belongs. I stand firm in my decision to honor and fulfill my desires, knowing nothing is too good to be true for me.

Rejoicing, I gratefully release this truth, joyously accepting my increasing good. I expand my sense of self. And so it is.

"We should expect the best, and so live that the best may become a part of our experience."

Ernest Holmes, *The Science of Mind*

I Expect the Best

Knowing I am one with the One Power and Presence as an individualization of It, I rejoice in this truth which sets me free to choose, expect, and create the very best in my life. As I wisely set my priorities, I trust in the Divine Law to support and execute what I choose. My intuition constantly guides me as I easily accomplish whatever is necessary for Spirit to work through me in manifesting my choices.

I boldly dismiss any thoughts or feelings that hold even the slightest hint of fear or uncertainty. Understanding that everything in my life is subject to change according to my thoughts and feelings, I sustain a clear consciousness of healthy expectancy for a life filled with joy, love, peace, prosperity, optimal health, and boundless creativity. Realizing that nothing is too good to be true for me, I choose, expect, and create the very best as my ongoing lifestyle. As I naturally expect the best, I so live that the best now becomes my experience.

Grateful that this is the way of my life, I release this truth into Divine Mind, knowing it is now so. I expect the best. And so it is.

"Never fear to be yourself... with the knowledge that the true self includes the inner and higher self which is always in immediate touch with the Great Divine Mind."

Thomas Troward,
The Edinburgh Lectures on Mental Science

I Express My True Self

I recognize the Great Divine Mind—the One Power and Presence of All that is—as Creator and Sustainer of the One Life, everywhere present in its entirety. As an individualized expression of this One Life, I know my true self is always in immediate touch with the Great Divine Mind, at all times and in all ways. I am a unique manifestation of Spirit through which Life flows.

Dismissing any conscious or subconscious patterns of unworthiness into the nothingness where they belong, I focus on a new awareness of unlimited opportunities which lie open to me. As I increasingly grow in awareness of my true self, I unfold more and more of my unlimited potential, expressing with confidence the uniqueness of who I am. I expand my sense of self and enlarge my sense of purpose as I easily and peacefully move forward to new heights of living.

Knowing I am worthy of my Divine nature, I joyfully and freely express my true self in all areas of my life. Rejoicing that this is so, I let it be. And so it is.

"Bless what you are, what you have, or you shall be less than you are... Bless or be less! Be no less than magnificent, no less than perfect, no less than Divine."

Dr. Tom Costa, *Life! Wanna Make Something of It?*

I Gratefully Bless All

Knowing I am an individuation of the One Power and Presence, I rejoice in the realization that I am no less than magnificent, no less than perfection, and no less than Divine.

As I bless what I am and what I have, I create a receptive, magnetic energy that naturally attracts increased blessings to me. These expansive blessings show up as optimal and vibrant health, unlimited and opulent supply, boundless and joyous creativity, and harmonious loving relationships. By agreeing with and blessing the events of my life, I do not resist any effects I have created by my previous thoughts and feelings. Affirming that only good comes from everything, I lovingly and gratefully bless all, creating more blessings for myself and others.

In the gratitude of knowing that these truths are now completed in Divine Mind, I release them as I allow their reality to manifest through me. I gratefully bless all, and I am blessed by all. And so it is.

"'Do you know what you are?' Spanish cellist Pablo Casals asks. 'You are a marvel, you are unique. In all the world there is no other... exactly like you.' Sing your unique song with gusto. And remember the advice of the Bal Shem Tov, a Jewish mystic, 'Compare not yourself with anybody else lest you spoil God's curriculum.'"

Frederic and Mary Ann Brussat,
Spiritual Literacy: Reading the Sacred in Everyday Life

I Honor and Express My Uniqueness

Recognizing the One Power and Presence of the Universe and knowing It is individualized as me in Its entirety, I delight in honoring and expressing the uniqueness of who I am.

In this unity consciousness I stay true to the authenticity of my individualized Self, easily and effectively contributing my part to make the world a better place. I embrace purposeful living in all areas of my life, and it shows up as boundless creativity, loving relationships, opulent supply, and optimal health. Generously and effortlessly, I lovingly give of my unique wisdom, appreciating and sharing the God-seed that I am.

Grateful for fulfilling my part in creating and sustaining a world that works peacefully and joyously for everyone, I release this truth and allow it to be. I honor and express my uniqueness, and so it is.

"Most people consider life a battle, but it is not a battle, it is a game."

Florence Scovel Shinn, *The Game of Life and How to Play It*

I Joyfully Play the Game of Life

Knowing that the One Power and Presence is expressing in Its entirety in me, through me, and as me, I give thanks that Life supports me as I joyfully, lovingly, and wisely play the game of Life.

As my understanding expands and my insights come from a deeper knowing, I increasingly embrace the truth that I am one with spiritual causation as It expresses through Universal Law.

There is no fear, confusion, or resistance in my consciousness. I am clear within my understanding as I live in faith, clarity and nonresistance. In conscious cooperation I wisely set my intentions. As I give attention to my intentions, I create new beginnings, causing expanded and unlimited potential to express in my life without any sense of battle, struggle, strain, or delay.

Trusting in the natural workings of the Law of Mind, I rejoice in seeing my desires easily manifest in wondrous and perfect ways in all areas of my life.

I give thanks as I fully accept this truth of my being. I joyfully, lovingly, and wisely play the game of Life. And so it is.

"Look around you right now. Quick! Find something to appreciate. SHAZAM! You're in the moment. Think of something in the future you're worried about... Think of something from the past you feel guilty over. Look around you right now. Quick! Find something to appreciate. SHAZAM! You're in the moment."

Gregg Sanderson,
Spirit with a Smile: The World According to BOB

I Joyfully Live in This Present Moment

Recognizing there is One Power and Presence in this eternal moment and knowing It expresses in, through, and as me in Its entirety, I delight in being one with It.

In the consciousness of this unity, I speak my word that I live joyfully in this moment and each moment as I evolve in my perfect unfolding of Spirit personified. Appreciating and being grateful for my life and all it encompasses, I thrive in the power of now. In this sacred awareness I easily and effectively create and sustain a consciousness of optimal health, opulent prosperity, boundless creativity, and loving relationships.

Knowing there is no power in the past or future, I keep my focus centered in the Infinite Potential of this moment. Grateful for knowing this is true for me, I release this truth in confidence and expectation of perfect results. I joyfully live in this present moment. And so it is.

"When we seek to deny or repress the drive toward our true potential, it is often because allowing our Divine nature to express itself involves the change that comes with growth and expansion... But the very nature of our lives challenges us to let go of who we thought we were and allow ourselves to be carried into the unknown."

Christina Grof, *The Thirst for Wholeness*

I Joyously Embrace My Divine Potential

Knowing I am an individualization of the One Power and Presence, I easily and naturally embrace my Divine Potential, allowing it to expand through greater and greater avenues of expression.

As I stay connected with the Creative Source of All-Being, I now make changes that bring spiritual growth and expansion into my consciousness, moving me into the unknown of my true potential.

I do not limit myself by any conscious or unconscious restrictive beliefs. Releasing anything and everything that is not harmonious with my new sense of self, I step forward in faith, trusting the Law of Mind to provide me with productive ideas, expansive vision, and delightful ways as I fulfill my Divine Potential.

Grateful that this is now true for me, I allow it to be. I joyously embrace my Divine Potential, and so it is.

"How to liberate this imprisoned splendor, by what means to discover the secret of release? 'There is a way,' the still small voice whispers, 'a way of surrender and listening.'"

Thomas Sannar, *The Power of Vow*

I Joyously Express My Inner Splendor

Knowing I am one with the One Power and Presence, I constantly live in the realization of this unity, honoring the Divine within myself and all others.

Living consciously in the present moment, I wake up to my inner splendor, allowing It to express freely, without hesitation or fear. Understanding there are no limitations in Divine Mind, I see only unlimited potential awaiting my intentions. I courageously move forward in my spiritual evolution, listening and surrendering to the whispers of the small, still voice within my consciousness. Following my inner wisdom I wisely and lovingly do that which is for my highest good and the highest good for all. As I live from the God nature within me, I naturally and easily bring forth my unique talents in ways that enrich, uplift, and inspire all in my world to live harmoniously in authenticity, kindness, and balance.

Grateful that this is the truth of my being, I release it unto the Law, knowing it is now so. I joyously express my inner splendor. And so it is.

"Call it conscience, intuition, or what we will, it is there. No [one] need go unguided through life, for all are Divine at the center and all are images of the Most High!"

Ernest Holmes, *Science of Mind*

I Listen to My Intuition

I joyously celebrate my oneness with the One Power and Presence—the all-powerful, all-prevailing and all-knowing essence of Life. I am alive and well, being fed from the Source. The stream of All-Consciousness flows to, through, and as me.

Knowing and feeling my oneness with this supreme all-encompassing Wisdom of the Universe, I now confidently and intelligently move forward into increased knowingness and greater awareness of the Divine Being that I am. In tune with my Divine center, I listen to my intuition and without hesitation follow its promptings. I am open to Spirit as It offers me wonderful pearls of wisdom. Listening and acting on this Divine wisdom, I am guided into right thinking and right action, clearly knowing and effectively doing what is the best in all situations of my life.

Grateful that this is now my natural way of living, I release this truth and know it is completed in Divine Mind. I let it be so and so it is.

"We must divest ourselves of all superstition, and know within ourselves that the Law of Life is not to be approached with fear and trembling, It is our servant, and we may confidently direct it into action in the specific field upon which our choice has fallen."

Fredrick Bailles, *Your Mind Can Heal You*

I Live Fearlessly

Knowing there is One Power and Presence and realizing I am an individualized expression of It, I move forward fearlessly in my living, loving, and being. In this consciousness of unity, I declare I am free and unlimited in my perception and reality of life.

There is nothing that can bind me or enclose me in self-defeating attitudes or habits. I easily dismiss any thoughts supporting limiting beliefs. My mind is now clear in full acceptance of the truth of my being, and I relax in the certainty of knowing there is no opposition to that which I present to the Law of Life. I now accept total freedom to follow my desires, knowing they are nudges of Spirit letting me know how I can move into my greater good. As I claim my fulfilled desires, I move fearlessly into the reality of their manifestation.

Grateful that this truth is now completed in Divine Mind, I release it, and let it be so. I live fearlessly. And so it is.

" ...first form the ideal conception of our object with the universal mind... and then affirm that our knowledge of the Law is sufficient reason for a calm expectation of a corresponding result. We can then turn to the affairs of our daily life with the calm assurance that the initial conditions are either there already or will soon come into view."

Thomas Troward, *The Edinburgh Lectures of Mental Science*

I Live in Calm Assurance

There is One Power and Presence permeating everything in the Universe. I rejoice that I am an individualized expression of It as It moves in Its entirety in, through, and as me.

I clarify my desired intentions, wisely choosing those that nurture and uplift me and all others in my world. Cooperating with the Intelligence of the Universe, I live in right action, able and willing to make any necessary changes so that the manifestations easily and peacefully work through me.

In calm assurance, I go about my daily life knowing that my declared intentions are now complete in Divine Mind and appear in due time in my world of effects.

Grateful that this is the truth of my being, I completely release any concern or anxiety as I trust the Law to creatively and intelligently respond to my truth. I live in calm assurance. And so it is.

"I can see clearly now. The rain is gone... Look all around, there's nothing but blue skies. Look straight ahead, nothing but blue skies... a bright, bright, sunshiny day."

Johnny Nash

I Live in Clarity and Right Action

There is One Power and Presence in the Universe. I delight in knowing and realizing that It expresses in, through, and as me in Its entirety. In the consciousness of this unity, I speak my word that I, now and always, live naturally in clarity and right action.

Honoring the magnificence of who I am, I purposely set my attention on my intentions as I easily, efficiently, and effectively accomplish what I choose to bring forth in my life. There is not a hint of delay, discord, or disruption as I peacefully live in right action in all areas of my life. I naturally make wise choices that sustain the perfect health of my body, my finances, my creativity, and my relationships. Knowing nothing is too good to be true for me, I expand my vision to vistas of new opportunities for increased good, lovingly filling myself and generously overflowing to those in my world.

Grateful for the reality of this truth, I release and let it go, knowing it is so now. I live in clarity and right action. And so it is.

"Get ready my soul, I'm diving in to the deepest kind of love, to the sweetest kind of life… Everything I've ever dreamed has brought me here to the present moment, here to a new beginning… and I'm seeing life so clearly now…"

Daniel Nahmod, *Get Ready My Soul*

I Live in Divine Clarity

Recognizing the One Power and Presence and diving deeper into the realization and awareness of my unity with Source, I see clearly that I am an individualized expression of the One Life.

I now experience increased understanding of my purpose of Being. I know who I am and what I am here to do. I naturally, peacefully, and willingly move forward in my spiritual evolution, trusting Universal Law to manifest what I present to It. Keeping my thoughts and feelings now and always perfectly aligned with my innermost desires, I welcome the perfect effects as they readily appear in my experience. As I live on purpose for my Divine callings, Spirit easily and effectively flows in, within, and as me, and I generously give my highest and best to the world.

Living in deeper awareness and realization of Spirit expressing as me, I gratefully release this truth, rejoicing that it is now so. I live in Divine clarity. And so it is.

"The Universe, both visible and invisible, is a Spiritual System. Man[kind] is a part of this Spiritual Order, so indivisibly united with It that the entire Cosmos is (or may be) reflected in [Its] mind!"

Ernest Holmes, *The Science of Mind*

I Live in Divine Order

In awe, I behold the Divine Order of the Universe. In appreciation, I recognize my oneness with It. I marvel at the Intelligence that creates and sustains in perfect patterns of unity all that exists throughout the Cosmos. I am a part of the Cosmos and an individualized expression within this perfect unity, reflecting Its perfect patterns in my life.

Joyfully accepting that I am a reflection of perfection, I bring my whole world of experience into focus with the whole, perfect manifestation of Divine order and right action. Any hints of disorder, disease or distress are dismissed as the untruths that they are. Keeping my focus on peace, joy, order, prosperity and love, I create and sustain everything in my life as a clear and accurate mirror of the perfect patterns of Divine Order. I am a living reflection of the pattern of perfection.

Trusting the workings of Universal Law, I gratefully release this truth, knowing it is now completed in Divine Mind. I live in Divine Order, and all is well. And so it is.

"Your Divine Potential is the fullest expression of your Spirit; it is discovering the depths of your capacity to create and to express love, compassion, forgiveness, generosity, and wisdom."

Caroline Myss,
Sacred Contracts: Awakening your Divine Potential

I Live in Divine Potential

Knowing the One Presence and Power permeates the entire Universe, I rejoice as I realize I am an individualized expression of It. In the felt consciousness of this unity, I affirm that I increasingly live in my Divine Potential, ever awakening to Its presence in, through, and as me.

By listening to my intuition—the Divine Presence within me—I easily and effectively discover the limitless depths of my capacity to create and to express love, compassion, forgiveness, generosity, and wisdom. Naturally and joyously experiencing the fullest expression of Spirit living as me, I wisely create and sustain wondrous and opulent effects in my life.

In harmony with the full flow of the Life Force of the Universe, I act courageously and confidently as I increasingly unfold and celebrate the wondrous spiritual qualities within me. I am the full expression of Spirit, lovingly moving forward to help make the world a better place. Grateful this truth is now manifested, I release it and allow it to be. I live in Divine Potential. And so it is.

"And there it is, a God-given calling, and you're running in the other direction flapping your wings instead of catching a thermal. I'm determined to hang out and catch more thermals."

Joan Borysenko,
Fried: Why You Burn Out and How to Survive

I Live in Ease and Grace

I rejoice that the One Power and Presence is individualized as me. It is who I am as I live, move, and have my being in ease and grace.

With every fiber of my being perfectly tuned to the Intelligence of the Universe, I allow my receptive nature to embrace the oneness of Life in its totality. I wisely cooperate as I do my part to uplift through wondrous ways the awakening of myself and all others to their inherent spiritual magnificence. I easily and graciously move in the direction of my God-given callings, feeling the joy and lightness of catching a thermal as I peacefully and effortlessly flow into my Infinite Potential.

Grateful for this truth of my being, I rejoice knowing I live in ease and grace. And so it is.

"We should approach the Law normally and naturally and with a sense of ease."

Ernest Holmes, *The Science of Mind*

I Live in Ease

I am one with the One Power and Presence. My life and Its life is the same life. In this consciousness of oneness I proclaim my life as a life of ease.

I allow not even a hint of discord, disaster, disorder, or disease, however subtle, to enter my realm of thinking. Letting go of any conscious or unconscious thoughts suggesting that struggle, strain, and challenge are in the slightest way necessary or beneficial to my spiritual evolution, I now create and sustain a life of peace, calm, and ease. I move forward joyfully, delightfully, and easily in my spiritual unfolding, knowing that the Creative Intelligence of the Universe brings into manifestation that which I impress upon It.

Thinking intelligently and staying in alignment with my choice of living in ease, I now relax, knowing that this Truth is firmly established and completed in Divine Mind. Giving thanks that this is so, I allow it to be. And so it is.

"I AM the sufficiency of my Universe. It is my decree. The elixir of beauty, of prospering effort, spreads forth from me. This is my irresistible, unending ministry. I think this—I speak this—I write this—I live this."

Emma Curtiss Hopkins, *The Radiant I AM*

I Live in Endless Sufficiency

The One Power and Presence now and forever expresses as, through, and in me as endless sufficiency. In the unity of this consciousness I fearlessly and adamantly decree there is always more than enough good to go around for all people.

Any thoughts, feelings, or actions resembling even a hint of insufficiency, lack, or limitation are easily and peacefully dissipated into the nothingness where they belong. There is no poverty, no want, or disappointed effort from this day forward.

My prospering thoughts, words, and actions effectively go forth from me to increase the sufficiency of good to all. My opulent consciousness naturally ripples out to effectively influence and prosper my world and the greater world of effects.

Grateful that this truth is now firmly established in Mind, I release it, knowing all are prospered in all ways from this day on. I live in endless sufficiency. And so it is.

"What is it that you tend to tackle with spontaneous mindfulness, so that without effort your whole heart is in it? ...You find meaning in it—not a meaning you could spell out in words, but meaning in which you can rest."

David Steindl-Rast, *Gratefulness, the Heart of Prayer*

I Live in Heartfelt Gratitude

The One Expression of Life is individualized as my life. It is through Its expression that I live, move, and have my being.

In tune with the unique essence of who I am, I gratefully embrace what has heart and meaning in my life. I live by resounding with the unique heartbeat of my life as I spontaneously resonate to the Divine essence of the harmony of my being. I effortlessly find meaning in which I can rest, assured all are blessed as I allow Life to flow through me in Its highest and best magnificent expression.

As I am filled with joyous life, this fullness naturally and generously overflows to my world, radiating the wondrous gifts of Spirit's presence. Knowing there is nothing to impede this unending flow of Life expressing through, in, and as me, I gratefully release this truth and joyously express the unique essence of who I am. I live in heartfelt gratitude. And so it is.

"The Mind of God is Infinite. The mind of man[kind] is some part of this Infinite, Creative Mind of God. Therefore the mind of man[kind] is as infinite as is man[kind's] capacity to understand his [or her] true relationship to God or Spirit."

Ernest Holmes, *The Science of Mind*

I Live in Infinite Potential

In the awareness of oneness with the One Power and Presence, I live in the consciousness of Infinite Potential, opening my mind to new vistas of living.

As I align my thoughts and feelings with expanded possibilities, I allow myself to see new visions and new ways of being in the world. I am now open to Infinite Mind moving through, in, and as me, creating within me a greater consciousness of peace, harmony, joy, creativity, prosperity, and love.

Knowing that I live in Infinite Potential, I refuse to accept any limiting ideas of myself or others. I gently embody my new world in ease and grace without any sense of struggle or strain.

As I live in my ever-expanding potential, I joyously embrace the delightful effects of my new thinking as it shows up in my world. Accepting this truth as being completed in Divine Mind, I gratefully let it be so. And so it is.

"...time is not a thing of itself. It is simply a measure of experience in eternity. It is impossible to measure time; for yesterday is gone and tomorrow has not come, and today is rapidly slipping past. If we were to attempt to put a finger on any period of time, it would be gone before we could point to it."

Ernest Holmes, The Science of Mind

I Live in Limitless Time

In this moment of timeless eternity, I acknowledge the One Power and Presence as It exists in Its entirety in everything that is. As I embrace the realization of my individualization of Spirit, I move into a greater understanding of who I am—a powerful, magnificent being expressing the Divine in, through, and as me.

Knowing that time is not a thing of itself, I now transcend any false belief that there is not enough time for me to do the things I desire. I now easily accomplish whatever is necessary to live a purposeful and enjoyable life without feeling any pressure or limitations. All good is mine now in every moment, without delay and without hesitation.

Grateful that this is true for me, I rejoice as I know it is now completed in Divine Mind. I live in limitless time. And so it is.

"Wouldn't it be wonderful if we could cover the world in the most beautiful of water crystals? How do we go about this? The answer is love and gratitude... If all the people of the world can have love and gratitude, the pristine beauty of the earth will once again return."

Masaru Emoto, *The Hidden Messages in Water*

I Live in Love and Gratitude

Knowing that all living things exist in a constantly changing state of interconnectedness, and knowing that I am a living influence in the unity of the One Whole, I set my positive intent to live as a spiritual center of love and gratitude, radiating through my consciousness a positive effect upon the world.

Anything unlike the harmony of love and gratitude is totally and peacefully dismissed into the nothingness where it belongs. I lay no claim to that which is less than the highest spiritual perfection expressing as my life. As I exude the consciousness of love and gratitude, I live my life to the fullest, naturally and joyously expressing who I am—the perfect personification of unconditional love and unlimited gratitude.

Grateful to the Law which now accepts and manifests this positive intention, I relax into knowing my loving and grateful way of living contributes to upholding the pristine beauty of the world. I live in love and gratitude. And so it is.

"A new species is arising on the planet. It is arising now, and you are it."

Eckhart Tolle, *A New Earth*

I Live in Newness

Recognizing the One Power and Presence eternally expressing Itself in Its entirety in all creation, I joyfully embrace the truth that I am an individualization of It. In this blessed unity I set my intention to live in the newness of each moment, constantly being aware of who I truly am.

The Self I am now emerges into a new dimension of consciousness—one of enlightenment, liberation, awakening, and a greater sense of my life's purpose. Rising above any sense of limitation or fear, I confidently, easily, and peacefully experience an inner shift of consciousness, transcending undesirable or outdated conditions or circumstances. My inner shift of consciousness produces a new reality, a new earth. I awaken to a greater sense of my life's purpose as I embrace the truth of my being. I am the Light of consciousness; I am a field of conscious Presence. Not bound by the events of the past or the unknown of the future, the word I speak is now firmly rooted in the fertile soil of the subjectivity of Universal Law.

In gratitude, I release this truth into Universal Mind from which all things emerge. I live in newness. And so it is.

"The spiritual [person] needs no healing, health is an omnipresent reality, and when the obstructions that hinder healing are removed, it will be found that health was there all the time. So in your work, do not feel that you must heal anyone. Your only responsibility is to uncover the Truth."

Ernest Holmes, *The Science of Mind*

I Live in Optimal Health

Recognizing the One Power and Presence is all there is, I joyfully unify with It in Its entirety.

In this consciousness of unity I embrace the perfect expression of who I am—an individualized expression of the One.

I allow this perfection to express fully in, through, and as me as perfect health. Every cell in my body is functioning perfectly, resulting in perfect assimilation, perfect circulation, and perfect elimination. My life is one of energetic vitality, expressing in balance, harmony, and peace. Keeping my consciousness clear of any disturbance, I allow nothing to interfere with the perfect workings of my mind, emotions, and body. Every part of my body continually regenerates, keeping perfect harmony and balance as the natural state of my being and showing up in my world of effects as unbounded vitality and free flowing energy.

Grateful that this is now so, I release this truth as it manifests in my life. I live in optimal health. And so it is.

"When we create peace and harmony and balance in our minds, we will find it in our lives."

Louise Hay, *You Can Heal Your Life*

I Live in Peace, Harmony, and Balance

There is One Presence in the Universe, and It expresses Itself through, in, and as me. In this consciousness of oneness, I now claim my Divine right to a life filled with peace, harmony, and balance.

Staying clear about what I desire, I steadfastly refuse to accept any confusion or discord in my life. Knowing that I am co-creator with the One Power and Presence, I keep my thoughts and actions in alignment with what I desire. As I delight in cooperating with the laws of the Universe, I now create and sustain a life that is centered in peace, harmony, and balance.

I gratefully release my word to the Law of the Universe, knowing that it is now completed in Divine Mind. And so it is.

"As soon as you trust yourself, you will know how to live."

Johann Wolfgang Von Goethe

I Live in Self-trust

Knowing I am an individualized expression of the One Power and Presence in Its entirety, I live in total self-trust as I allow the uniqueness of Spirit to express in, through, and as me. As I listen to the inner voice of wisdom within me, I respond in right thinking and right action, trusting the intuitive leadings of Spirit to direct me in ways that are for the good of all.

Being free from any false beliefs of doubt, fear, or obstacles of any kind, I easily, peacefully, and intelligently follow the promptings of Spirit as It clearly and continually directs me into my highest and most purposeful life. I now unhesitatingly accept the infinite possibilities that await my recognition as I move forward joyously and fearlessly in the manifestation of my desires. I embrace and honor my self-knowing as I trust the truth of Spirit within me to express in loving and wondrous ways.

Rejoicing that this is now so, I release this truth, trusting Spirit as me to express magnificently in my world. I live in Self-trust. And so it now is.

"When we are spiritually fit and balanced we are a powerfully exquisite blend of human fallibility and Divine perfection. It is this dynamic tension that gives us our uniqueness, our power to create and our compassion."

Caroline Reynolds, *Spiritual Fitness*

I Live in Spiritual Fitness

From the place of knowing that I am a unique individualized expression of the One Divine Power and Presence, I confidently express this consciousness of unity, radiating love, compassion, kindness, and wisdom to myself and to all in my world.

As I live in alignment with my inner wisdom, I manifest clarity and creativity in all areas of my life. I bring forth the truth of who I am, trusting the Universe to support my expressions of authenticity and integrity. Following my inner knowing, I joyfully and easily now accept the manifestations of my intentions. I am at peace as all the events of my life unfold in balance and in perfect Divine Order, establishing and maintaining sacredness in my everyday life.

Grateful that this truth is now so for me, I rejoice in it and allow it to be. I live in spiritual fitness. And so it is.

"In sufficiency we recognize and celebrate money's power for good—our power to do good with it—and we can experience fulfillment in directing the flow toward our highest ideals and commitments."

Lynne Twist, *The Soul of Money*

I Live in Sufficiency

I fully realize and feel in every fiber of my being that I am an individualization of the One Power and Presence expressing in, through, and as me. In this consciousness of being one with the Source of All Good, I open myself to receive overflowing and opulent supply from the unlimited radiant Source of the One.

As I am filled by this Source, I generously allow It to overflow in all areas of my life. Any thoughts, feelings, or actions resembling even a hint of insufficiency, lack, or limitation are easily and peacefully dissipated into the nothingness where they belong. I stand firm in knowing I am sufficient in all ways. It is who I am, and I live steadfastly in this knowing. As I perceive the world as one in which there is always enough, I see myself as always being enough, creating and sustaining a natural and constant flow of money and all-sufficiency.

Joyfully and gratefully rejoicing in this truth, I allow it to be so. I live in sufficiency. And so it is.

"When you meditate, open not only your listening mind but the other door of your mind as well so that eternal love streams out as fast as it comes in."

Mary Strong, *Letters of the Scattered Brotherhood*

I Live in the Divine Flow of Life

I am one with the eternal stream of Life flowing throughout all existence. Living in the realization of this unity, I embrace who I am, rejoicing in the Presence of the Divine Flow of Life individualized in, through, and as me. In this sacred awareness, I now unhesitatingly move confidently forward in the perfect expression of right action. True to my God nature, I express love and light in ways that bless all.

Being led by Spirit to easily and courageously create the perfect world of effects, I allow no fear or doubt to enter my consciousness. My every action is sanctioned by Divine Source as I naturally and easily experience and express the eternal stream of love. I intelligently guide the direction of my talents to the highest and greatest good, joyfully offering uplifting and nurturing inspiration from the ever-flowing, constant current of Life.

Living in the Divine flow of Life, I joyously, freely, and lovingly express who I am. I rejoice in this truth, and let it be. And so it is.

"Giving is basically an attitude with which you touch things… there is a wellspring of life within you, and yours is the privilege at any time of giving way to its flow. If ever there is a lack of any kind… something is blocking the flow. Something's got to give!"

                        Eric Butterworth, *Spiritual Economics*

I Live in the Divine Flow of Spirit

Knowing there is One Power and Presence in all things, I rejoice that I am one with the One. In the consciousness of this unity, I declare that I, now and always, live harmoniously in the Divine flow of Spirit.

Giving and receiving is my natural way of living. It is the attitude with which I touch all people and all things in my life. There is no blockage of any kind hindering this flow. I gladly share the expression of my unique talents in all that I do, say, and think, giving freely and joyously of who I am and what I have. In each moment, I perceive new and grander avenues through which I increasingly experience the Divine flow of Spirit as I generously and willingly give of my talents, resources, love, and creativity.

Grateful that this is the truth of my being, I easily and peacefully release my word to Universal Law. I live in the Divine flow of Spirit. And so it is.

"Die to the past every moment. You don't need it. Only refer to it when it is absolutely relevant to the present. Feel the power of this moment and the fullness of Being. Feel your presence."

Eckhart Tolle, *The Power of Now*

I Live in the Now

In this moment I feel my fullness of Being. I know I am an individualized expression of the One Power and Presence; I am aware of my Divine nature.

Knowing and feeling this truth, I allow myself to be fully present in the now as I experience the flow of Spirit pulsing through me. Refusing to live in past thinking, I am open to the magnificence of each moment and each breath. Breathing in, I feel Spirit inspiring me. Breathing out, I release that which does not nurture me. I know that Spirit is closer to me than this very breath I now breathe, and I relax into the present reality of being one with the One. As I do, I experience greater receptivity and increased realization of my connection with the One Power and Presence expressing through All that is.

As I feel and know this Divine Presence within me, I joyfully release this truth, being grateful that it is so. I live in the now. And so it is.

"Out beyond ideas of wrongdoing and rightdoing, there is a field. I'll meet you there. When the soul lies down in that grass, the world is too full to talk about. Ideas, language, even the phrase 'each other' doesn't make any sense."

Rumi

I Live in the Oneness of Spirit

Spirit is all there is. There is no other. In this consciousness of sacred oneness, I gratefully recognize that I am an individualized expression of the One—the Creator and Sustainer of all Life. Knowing that this One Life permeates all there is, I am alive with Its presence as It expresses in, through, and as me in Its entirety. That which It is, I am.

I am grateful that this Divine oneness lovingly supports me in all areas of my life as I embrace the warmth and wisdom of Its Being. Easily, effectively, and intelligently I make wise choices that lead me to an expanded awareness of who I am. I welcome the effects of these choices as they show up in my life as love, wisdom, and joy. Knowing my interconnectedness with All-Good, I peacefully move forward in my spiritual evolution in harmony and wellbeing.

Grateful for knowing that this is the truth of me, I release it and allow it to be. I live in the oneness of Spirit, and so it is.

"Faith, conviction, and belief are real. Spiritual Power is not an illusion, and the world in which we live is the objective counterpart of a spiritual Reality. There is a deeper voice that speaks, beyond the experience, which causes us to know that we are eternal, immortal, and Divine."

Ernest Holmes, *Freedom from Stress*

I Live in the Reality of Spirit

There is One Power and Presence. It is the spiritual reality of which all things are formed, and It is the spiritual reality individualized as me. I am a living embodiment of It.

In the consciousness of this unity I rejoice knowing that faith, conviction, and belief are real. Any thought of spiritual power being an illusion is totally erased from my mind. I experience my world as the objective counterpart of embracing the reality of Spirit. I listen to the deeper voice that causes me to know I am eternal, immortal, and Divine. In this knowing I now and forever partake of the essence of Spirit, continually making all things new and wonderful as I create and sustain a world of increasing beauty, joy, love, and peace.

Grateful that this is so, I release this truth as I live in the reality of Spirit. And so it is.

"There is a Divine sequence running throughout the Universe… To come into harmony with it thereby with all the higher laws and forces is to come into the chain of this wonderful sequence. This is the secret of all success."

Ralph Waldo Trine, *In Tune With the Infinite*

I Live in Tune With the Infinite

There is One Power and Presence from which all things emerge. It is the Source of All Good and flows harmoniously in, through, and as me in Its entirety. I delight that I am an individualized expression of It.

Knowing the truth of my being, I live in harmony with this Divine sequence as I willingly and intelligently stay in tune with the Infinite. I totally and firmly dismiss any hint of discord, disharmony, disease, or disarray of any kind into the nothingness where it belongs. I embrace a life of joy, peace, love, prosperity, wholeness, and right action as I consciously direct the Infinite Potential within me to bring only good and greater good into my consciousness.

In gratitude, I generously allow It to overflow into the lives of all those in my world. Accepting that this truth is now real for me, I release it into the Law and let it be. I live in tune with the Infinite. And so it is.

"This is how creativity happens—when the mind is fertile; when everything is seen as having value and each event is welcomed as an opportunity; when strange and unforeseen accidents are met with confidence; when the unpredictable dance of life, rather than causing fear or annoyance, stimulates interest; and when there is always a 'why' to ask, always a game to play."

Piero Ferrucci, Inevitable Grace

I Live in Unlimited Creativity

Being one with the Creator of all things, I joyously individualize the ever-flowing, never-ending Life of unlimited creativity.

I keep my mind clear and fertile, seeing everything as having intrinsic value and every event as an uplifting opportunity. I easily and effectively dismiss any fears or annoyances that appear to be real as I openly embrace my infinite potential, intelligently creating beautiful and bold blessings for myself and all others. With undying confidence, I courageously and fearlessly meet all the effects appearing in my life, knowing that by applying my understanding of universal principles and by perfectly aligning my thoughts and feelings with my desires, I create new and wonderful experiences resulting in an expanded consciousness of increased opulence, peace, joy, and love.

Grateful that this is so, I rejoice as I release this truth into Divine Mind. I live in unlimited creativity. And so it is.

"Every time you are tempted to react in the same old way, ask if you want to be a prisoner of the past or a pioneer of the future. The past is closed and limited; the future is open and free."

Deepak Chopra

I Live in New Beginnings

God is the power of now—everywhere present in all manifestations. In this moment of sacred unity with the One Power and Presence, I rejoice as I now live, move, and have my being in new beginnings.

I wisely choose new intentions, intelligently cooperating with the Law of the Universe and staying in tune with my intuition as it guides me in the perfection of each new creation. Letting go of any thoughts or feelings, regrets or successes from the past, I live in the infinite potential of each and every moment, initiating new and glorious beginnings that are unprecedented and unlimited expressions of magnificence personified. I easily keep the focus of my attention on my intentions, creating and sustaining new and opulent experiences, blessing myself and all others.

Unfolding more and more to the Divine potential within me, I gratefully and joyously know this to be the truth of my being in each moment of my life. I live in new beginnings. And so it is.

"I am pure intelligence, acting intelligently."

Raymond Charles Barker, *The Power of Decision*

I Live Intelligently

There is One Power and Presence in the Universe expressing as all-knowing Omniscience, all-powerful Omnipotence and all-present Omnipresence. I am a unique individualized expression of this One Power and Presence as It moves through, in and as me.

In this consciousness of unity, everything I need to know to live my life intelligently is now revealed to me in clarity and with ease. As I recognize and implement the inner promptings of Spirit, I live decisively and wisely. Pure intelligence fills my entire being and manifests as right thinking and right action in all areas of my life. My creative expression flourishes in myriads of awesome wonder; my relationships bring joy to my heart; my physical body is filled with energy and balance; my world lovingly nurtures me and opulently supports me in all ways. As I increasingly expand my awareness of being pure intelligence, I invite ever greater new, nurturing and prosperous experiences into my life. I now delight in knowing that all I do automatically reflects the intelligence and wisdom of my Divine nature for I am pure intelligence, living intelligently.

I now gratefully release this truth into Divine Mind, rejoicing as I allow it to be. And so it is.

"A miracle is an ordinary event that lies outside your current structure of knowing. Rainer Maria Rilke once wrote: 'Whoever you are, some night step outside the house you know so well… enormous space is near.'"

Maria Nemeth, Ph.D., *The Energy of Money*

I Live Limitlessly

The all-knowing, all-powerful Presence in Its entirety permeates all that exists. It is limitless in Its being and in Its actions. As I am an individualized expression of It, I am limitless potential, envisioning and expanding the scope of my life beyond my current structures of knowing.

Willingly, wisely, and fearlessly I now move in the direction of my desires, releasing any ideas, thoughts, beliefs or habits that do not totally support me in my enhanced and expanded consciousness. Effortlessly I extend my structures of knowing, and I easily embrace increased financial prosperity, optimal wellness, boundless creativity and loving, nurturing relationships.

Trusting the Universe to support me as I wisely set my intentions, I now relax into the adventure of my ever-expanding life, accepting and welcoming the magnificence and opulence manifesting in, through, and as me.

Grateful that this is now so, I rejoice as I release this truth to Divine Mind, knowing it is done. I live limitlessly. And so it is.

"When we know our Oneness with God and Law, what a great burden is removed. Any sense of opposition is removed from the consciousness which perceives unity."

Ernest Holmes, *The Science of Mind*

I Live My Life Lightly

Knowing I am one with the Source of All Being, I now relax into trusting Creative Intelligence to bring forth in perfect ways all the good that I impress upon It.

I clear my consciousness of any burden of false responsibility that I must struggle to make the Law work. It naturally and easily creates for me as I allow It to work through me. Knowing this, I now consciously align my thoughts and feelings with my desires, thus setting the Law in motion and directing It toward my chosen manifestations. Appreciating and applying my understanding of this truth, I now move into greater experiences of joyous and opulent living. Filled and overflowing with laughter and love, I enjoy perfect health and prosperity as natural states of my consciousness as I express my Divine Self in magnificent myriads of wonder and awe.

Delighted that this is now true for me, I gratefully release any doubt or worry as I move through this day with lightness in my step and a smile in my heart. I live my life lightly. And so it is.

"…the word 'prosperity' in its root means 'wholeness'… the spiritual laws of wholeness, when practiced, bring peace, health and plenty into our lives."

Catherine Ponder, *The Dynamic Laws of Prosperity*

I Live Prosperously

The One Power and Presence is everywhere present in all Its totality. I am one with It. In this consciousness of unity, I am grateful Creative Intelligence easily and clearly demonstrates in perfect ways that which I impress upon It.

I now accept, without any obstruction or delay, a reality of prosperous living. Any thoughts in my conscious or unconscious mind that may negate the perfect manifestation of a joyous and opulent life are peacefully and completely dissolved into the nothingness where they belong. By cooperating with Spiritual Law, I maintain a consciousness of peace, health, and prosperity. My relationships are loving and supportive, my self-expression flows creatively and joyously, my supply is constant and abundant, and my health reflects perfect wholeness and wellbeing.

Grateful that my word is Truth, I rejoice as I allow it to be so. I live prosperously. And so it is.

"I think prosperity is about having 'enough'—having a life beyond need and worry. It's about more than prosperity in financial terms. It's more about being satisfied, about having a prosperous heart."

Julia Cameron, *The Prosperous Heart*

I Live with a Prosperous Heart

The One Power and Presence fills the Universe with Its eternal and Infinite essence. I live, move, and have my being in It as it expresses clearly, easily, and effectively through, in, and as me in Its entirety.

Satisfied with who I am, I effortlessly and wisely move peacefully forward with a prosperous and loving heart, embracing greater good in my life as I consciously nurture myself and generously allow the overflow to bless all those in my world. I delight in enjoying a life beyond need and worry; beyond any sense of struggle, strife or strain; beyond any concerns, doubts, or fears; beyond any limited thinking or beliefs; beyond even the slightest hint of a possible lack of supply. I naturally attract loving relationships, boundless creativity, increased financial wealth, and vibrant, perfect health.

I confidently release this truth to the Law knowing my desires on every level are easily manifested now and always in perfect ways. For this I am truly grateful. I live with a prosperous heart, and so it is.

"Yea, though I walk through the valley of the shadow of death, I will fear no evil; for Thou art with me... Surely Thy goodness and mercy shall follow me all the days of my life, and I will dwell in the house of the Lord forever."

                              Psalm 23, Lamsa edition, *The Holy Bible*

I Lovingly Nurture Myself

Spirit is all there is, and I am an individualization of It. In the stillness of this eternal moment, I allow It to express in Its entirety through, in, and as me. It is who I am.

In the consciousness of this unity, I bask in the warmth of courting the Presence, rejoicing as I feel the surety of It upholding me in all ways. Grateful that Universal Law is ever present as It conspires to lovingly support me, I easily and effectively move in the direction of my desires. In calm assurance I surrender to my highest and best life as I trust my inner knowing to lead me on the paths of peaceful and purposeful living.

Delighted and grateful that this is now the truth of my being, I release this prayer to Universal Law as I ease into this day and every day, lovingly nurturing myself all the way. And so it is.

"Decision is the most important function of the individual mind. No creative process can begin until a decision is made… Having made the decision, every right idea will flow into my consciousness. Each idea will reveal itself at the instant I need it."

Raymond Charles Barker, *The Power of Decision*

I Make Up My Mind

There is One Mind, and I live, move, and have my being as an individualized expression of It. Its Mind and my mind are One Mind.

In the consciousness of this unity, I now make up my mind to live my life in perfect ways, resulting in blessings to myself and all beings. I honor my relationship to the oneness of all living things, nurturing all of creation in loving and peaceful ways. Keeping in mind that I am an important, essential part of the essence of all Life, I live so that I naturally give of my best to myself and to the world. Being mindful of my role in the Cosmic scheme of all things, I create and sustain a consciousness that increasingly touches all living creatures with love, peace, and joy.

Knowing this is good enough to be true for me, I release this truth, grateful that it is now firmly established in Divine Mind. My mind is made up. I live my life as a blessing to myself and to the world. And that's the way it is.

"No matter how limited your sphere of activities may seem to you and how small your town appears on the map, if you develop your mental and spiritual forces through love thoughts you can be a power to move the world along. Rise up and realize your strength."

Ella Wheeler Wilcox, *The Heart of New Thought*

I Realize My Spiritual Strength

Right now in this moment I know I am an individualization of the One Power and Presence. In the consciousness of this unity I am aware that Spirit expresses through me as wisdom, love, peace, joy, and right action. As I embrace this knowing, I rise up and realize my spiritual strength.

I rise above any thoughts defying my spiritual power and effectiveness as I stay centered in the truth of who I am—Spirit in form. I rise above any less than desirable circumstances in my life appearing as effects of less than desirable thinking. I now create the life I desire by keeping my focus on loving thoughts, wise actions, and clear intentions.

Aware of my spiritual magnificence, I increasingly awaken to my oneness with Spirit. I rise up and realize my spiritual strength, giving thanks that this is the truth of my being. I delight in letting it be so. And so it is.

"When you say 'yes' to what is, you become aligned with the power and intelligence of Life itself. Only then can you become an agent for positive change in the world."

Eckhart Tolle, *Stillness Speaks*

I Say Yes to Life

Recognizing the One Power and Presence as all that is, I delight in knowing I am one with It as It individualizes in, through, and as me in Its entirety. In the consciousness of this unity, I adamantly and unhesitatingly resound forth a huge YES to Life.

By saying yes to my life as it is, I am saying yes to the greater Life of all Being. Bringing my entire focus into alignment with the awesome power and Creative Intelligence of the Universe, I become a more effective agent for positive change in the world. Any thought of discord, disease, or doubt is now dissipated into the nothingness where it belongs. I openly and lovingly embrace the positive as my way of living. Keeping my purpose clearly attuned to the harmony of all things, I create and sustain the perfect effects of a world that works beautifully for everyone.

Grateful for the reality of this truth, I release it knowing it now shows up in my world. I say yes to Life. And so it is.

"Stop swimming so hard, and climb in the boat with Noah."

Rumi, *This Longing*
(Translation, Coleman Barks & John Moyne)

I Simplify and Glorify My Life

I am one with Divine Mind. As such, I am a part of the ever-present, ever-precise workings of Universal Law. In the consciousness of oneness with the all-pervading Divine Spirit, I rest in total confidence and faith that my desires are the right action of Universal Intelligence. I trust Spirit to guide and support me in everything that is good and right for me.

I now establish in my mind, and therefore into Divine Mind, my desire to both simplify and glorify my life. I joyfully accept an environment of order and beauty. Anything not supporting my highest expression of life is gently released from my consciousness as I move into a greater and greater sense of lightness and ease in living. As I simplify and glorify my life, I am clear about my priorities, and my life reflects my clear thinking.

Knowing that my desire is now completed in Divine Mind, I gratefully allow it to be, and so it is. All is well.

"We are all prisoners of our own mind. This realization is the first step in the journey to freedom."

Ram Dass

I Step Boldly into Freedom

In awe, I recognize the One Power and Presence as all-powerful, all-knowing, and everywhere-present in Its entirety. As It naturally and effectively expresses in, through, and as me, I rejoice knowing I am an individualized expression of It.

In the consciousness of this unity I step boldly into freedom. I courageously claim freedom from stress, freedom from lack, freedom from any false beliefs, and freedom from any sense of separation from my Source. I courageously and joyously embrace and express the freedom to live in unlimited and opulent ways that sustain increased love, peace, creativity and prosperity in all areas of my life. In this consciousness of freedom rising from my soul, I am increasingly aware of new and expansive ideas and my Infinite potential. Knowing the Universe lovingly conspires to support me in my chosen intentions, I delight in trusting Creative Intelligence to creatively and intelligently perform in wondrous ways, bringing about my heartfelt desires into visible and recognizable manifestations.

In gratitude I release this truth into the Law, knowing it is done. I step boldly into freedom. And so it is.

"Wherever we have drawn the line, the risk of crossing it feels very real."

  Oriah Mountain Dreamer, *The Invitation*

I Stretch My Spiritual Muscles

Totally present in Its entirely in all people, places, and things, the One Power and Presence expresses in, through, and as me. I am an individualized expression of Spirit, and I joyously celebrate this Truth.

In this consciousness of unity, I determine what takes place in my everyday living and wisely plan for my future. Aware that my mind is one with Divine Mind, I consciously decide what goes into my subconscious; I think only of what I want and produce only what I want. I cooperate by allowing right thinking to fill my consciousness. There is no room for confusion, indecision, or procrastination. Keeping my focus on clarity, decisiveness, and right action, I easily manifest my desires. Knowing nothing is too good to be true, I stretch my spiritual muscles to embody more of my unlimited potential, bringing expanded possibilities into manifestation. I graciously accept the best for myself and generously give my best to the world.

In gratitude, I release this Truth and allow it to be. And so it is.

"...a hunch or an inner prompting simply indicates that the good which you desire actually desires to be yours. Desire is God tapping at the door of your mind, trying to give you greater good. That you deeply desire something is positive proof that it has already been prepared for you and is only waiting for you to recognize and accept it."

    Catherine Ponder, *The Dynamic Laws of Prosperity*

I Wisely Follow My Intuition

The One Power and Presence is everywhere present in Its entirety. I am an individualized expression of It as it lives in, through, and as me.

In the consciousness of this unity, I easily recognize and readily accept the manifestations of my innermost desires. Knowing nothing is too good to be true, I clearly and willingly give attention to my chosen intentions as I gratefully see them effortlessly and quickly appear in my life. I refuse to think of my desired good as being apart from me or being difficult to obtain. In faith and confidence I use my ideas and inner feelings to create a more wonderful world for myself and others.

In gratitude I now joyously embrace the reality of my desires in this present moment. I wisely follow my intuition. And so it is.

"Before you agree to do anything that might add even the smallest amount of stress to your life, ask yourself: What is my truest intention? Give yourself time to let a 'Yes!' resound within you. When it's right, I guarantee that your entire body will feel it."

Oprah Winfrey

I Wisely Set My Truest Intentions

I recognize the One Power and Presence expressing in, through, and as me. In this sacred unity of consciousness I resound to Spirit as It shows up in my life as wisdom and right action.

I wisely set my truest intentions, allowing nothing to distract or disturb me from giving them my undivided attention. I am led by Spirit to easily accomplish all things necessary for the fulfillment of my desires. Knowing that each time I focus my attention I create a new beginning, I am confident that new and wonderful ways of living appear as present realities in my life. Living in clarity of purpose, I keep my focus on my highest priorities as I intelligently and peacefully move in the direction of my goals, accepting them as already completed in the absolute realm of Divine Mind.

Grateful that this truth now exists for me, I release it to Universal Law, knowing it is manifested. I wisely set my truest priorities. And so it is.

"Congratulations! Today is your day. You're off to great places! You're off and away! You have brains in your head. You have feet in your shoes. You can steer yourself any direction you choose!"

Dr. Suess, *Oh, The Places You'll Go!*

I Wisely Steer Myself Toward My Greater Good

Knowing the One Power and Presence is all there is, I rejoice in the realization that It expresses through, in, and as me in Its entirety. In the consciousness of this unity, I delight in easily, effectively, and wisely steering myself toward my greater good.

I claim this day as mine to set my heart and mind as the compass to lead me in the direction of new, fulfilling, and nurturing experiences. As I courageously and decisively release old patterns of thoughts and habits that have kept me in worn out situations, I openly embrace new expansive beliefs and visions that uplift me into the greater good of lavish prosperity, boundless creativity, optimal health, and radiant happiness. Today is the day, now is the time, and I am the person to experience increased awareness of my spiritual magnificence. I'm off to great places as I create new and joyous ways of living.

Accepting this truth as my reality, I gratefully release it and allow it to be. I wisely steer myself toward my greater good. And so it is.

"Your prayer, your desire, and your inner urge are like a magnet and the stronger they are, the stronger the power of your magnet and the greater its attraction. You cannot ask too much of the Law, for it is unlimited and the supply is inexhaustible."

Raymond Holliwell, *Working with the Law*

I Wisely Work with the Law

Acknowledging the One Power and Presence manifesting as All-Good, I rejoice that I am an individualized expression of It. In this consciousness of unity, I affirm that I wisely work with the Law. I am a magnet for good and greater good.

Knowing my true desires represent the urge of Life seeking a fuller expression, I keep them alive by continuous expectation of fulfillment. I focus my attention on clear intentions, effective prayer, and loving thoughts, drawing to myself the manifestation of my desires. Giving the best of myself to Life, I receive the best of Life in return. I proceed without doubt or fear as I expect and accept all the good I can realize, use, and enjoy. Whatever I desire in health, success, happiness and prosperous living easily comes to me now through the natural principle of the Law.

Gratefully releasing this truth, I accept good and greater good in my life. I wisely work with the Law. And so it is.

"I know who I am and the odds are in my favor. Everything that happens to me happens for me. My life is unfolding perfectly no matter what. So let it!"

James Mellon, *Core Prosperity Relief*

My Life is Unfolding Perfectly

In awe I recognize and honor the One Power and Presence as all there is. I rejoice in knowing It is everywhere present in Its entirety individualized in, through, and as me. In the consciousness of this unity and in a deep sense of spiritual knowing, I rejoice that my life is now unfolding perfectly no matter what.

Anything seeming to appear as an obstacle is instantaneously dissipated into the nothingness where it belongs. There is not a hint of resistance, struggle, or strain in any way related to my perfect unfolding. Having set this intention, I now easily and clearly listen to my intuition as I effortlessly, peacefully, and wisely accomplish all things necessary for the fulfillment of this truth.

Grateful that this truth is now a present reality in my life, I unhesitatingly and joyfully release it to Universal Law and allow it to be. My life is unfolding perfectly no matter what. And so it is.

"Today is a good day for war to come to an end."

> Deepak Chopra, *Peace is the Way*

Peace Is My Way

As I live easily in harmonious oneness with the One Power and Presence, perfect peace naturally flows in, through, and as me.

In this consciousness of unity there is no room for anything unlike the full expression of peace. I allow not the slightest hint of any thought or feeling into my consciousness that entertains anything less than perfect peace. My life is one of harmony, lovingly and effectively expressing thoughts, feelings, and actions that reflect respect and the oneness of all living things. Through my personal transformation I consciously choose to contribute to the establishment and maintenance of peace in the world. Dedicating my life to peaceful living, I personify peace in all areas of my life. I keep my consciousness clear in knowing I am a center of peace. It is who I am, and it is my natural way of being.

In gratitude I release this truth into Divine Mind, knowing it is now manifested in me and in the world around me. Peace is my way. And so it is.

Part Four

APPENDICES

Create Your Own
Affirmative Prayer

Steps for Creating Your Own Prayer

Title:

Recognizing:

Unifying:

Accepting:

Denying Any Obstacle *(Optional):*

Reaffirming *(Optional):*

Expressing Gratitude:

Releasing:

A User-friendly Checklist
for Your Affirmative Prayers

___ Is my prayer written in the first person?
   (I, me, myself)

___ Is my prayer written in the present tense?
   (I now accept....)

___ Have I applied active voice throughout?
   (I release...)

___ Have I included all the affirmative prayer steps?

   Recognizing

   Unifying

   Accepting

   Denial and Reaffirmation *(if applicable)*

   Expressing Gratitude

   Releasing

___ Does my prayer flow from my heart with feelings that are now true for me?

A Reminder of Your Importance

"There is a vitality, a life force, an energy, a quickening that is translated through you into action, and because there is only one of you in all of time, this expression is unique. And if you block it, it will never exist through any other medium, and it will be lost. The world will not have it. It is not your business to determine how good it is, nor how valuable, nor how it compares with other expressions. It is your business to keep it yours clearly and directly, to keep the channel open. You do not even have to believe in yourself or your work. You have to keep yourself open and aware to the urges that motivate you. Keep the channel open."

Martha Graham, Choreographer

About the Author

Hi, I'm Nancy Fagen, and I'm glad you found me in the pages of *It's a Divine Done Deal!*

I live in St. Augustine, Florida, and serve as the senior minister of Center for Spiritual Living Jacksonville. I also teach spiritual psychology as adjunct faculty for the global distance learning program at Sofia University based in Palo Alto, California.

When I'm not being minister, teacher, or writer, some of my favorite things are walking on the beach, playing tennis, and being with my family and grandchildren.

I've written and published these affirmative prayers to share them with the world and present tools for you to write your own prayers. I trust my purpose is fulfilled.

Thank you for your interest in the content of this book. I affirm for you a deepening of your soul's journey as you easily and peacefully move forward in your spiritual evolution.

In spiritual support,
Nancy

Acknowledgements

When I was in the process of fulfilling requirements for ordination, my sponsor, Rev. Sandy Freeman-Loomis, suggested I write affirmative prayers, also called spiritual mind treatments, for *Creative Thought* magazine. I followed her suggestion, and my affirmative prayers began appearing in the magazine. Thank you, Sandy.

This led me to a friendship and working relationship with Rev. Dr. Cynthia Cavalcanti, who was editor of *Creative Thought*. Cynthia lovingly encouraged me with my writing, helping me birth my first book, *Divine Nudges of Spirit*, and leading me to my competent and cooperative editor, Denise O'Connor, for *It's a Divine Done Deal*. Thank you Cynthia and Denise!

I give a loud shout out of thanks to all those who supported and inspired me along the way. Most importantly, I gratefully acknowledge you, the readers, who continue to meet me in these pages. I honor your presence with me in this life journey and affirm that all your desires become Divine Done Deals!

Contact Information

Dr. Fagen is available for speaking engagements. facilitating workshops and personal consultations by telephone or skype. For a free chapter of this book and other valuable information, visit DivineDoneDeal.com or write the author at P. O. Box 565, St. Augustine, FL 32085.